W9-AQT-531

I AM A STRANGER ON THE EARTH

The Story of Vincent Van Gogh

Self-portrait of Vincent Van Gogh

I AM A STRANGER ON THE EARTH

The Story of Vincent Van Gogh

BY ARNOLD DOBRIN

Frederick Warne & Co.   New York • London

ACKNOWLEDGMENTS

Van Gogh's paintings and drawings are reproduced by the
kind permission of the following: State Museum Kroller-Muller,
Otterlo, Netherlands; the Stedlijk Museum, Amsterdam;
the Museum of Modern Art, New York; the Fogg Museum,
Cambridge, Massachusetts; the Metropolitan Museum of Art,
New York; Yale University Art Gallery, New Haven, Connecticut;
and Mr. and Mrs. Leigh B. Block, Chicago, Illinois.

Copyright © Arnold Dobrin 1975
All Rights Reserved
Printed in the United States of America
LCC: 75-8105

Composition by Frost Bros., Inc.
Printing by Neff Lithographing Co., Inc.
Binding by A. Horowitz & Son

1   2   3   4   5   6   7   8   9   10

FOR BOB VARI

The quotations which accompany the artist's work were chosen to reflect Van Gogh's own view. Many of the quotations come from letters written later in life to his brother, Theo, and are excerpts from *The Complete Letters of Vincent Van Gogh* published by the New York Graphic Society, Greenwich, Connecticut.

TABLE OF CONTENTS

*"One cannot always tell what it is that keeps us shut in,
confines us, seems to bury us, but, however, one feels certain
barriers, certain gates, certain walls. Is all this imagination
fantasy? I do not think so. And then one asks: 'My God!
Is it for long, is it forever, is it for eternity?' Do you know what
frees one from this captivity? It is every deep serious
affection. Being friends, being brothers, love, that is what
opens the prison by supreme power, by some magic force."*

—Vincent Van Gogh

*"What beauty exists
in the face of a simple
peasant woman, tired and poor
though she may be ..."*

1. BOYHOOD IN THE NETHERLANDS

Well over a hundred years ago a small boy ran through the moist fields and woods of Brabant in the southern Netherlands. He loved the fresh, clean wind on his face; he loved to watch the swiftly moving clouds swirling in from the North Sea. And the hidden joys of nature, the peasants at work and at rest—all the wonders of the natural world were, to him, remarkable beyond words. The boy's name was Vincent Van Gogh. He was born March 30, 1853.

Vincent's home life—in the small village of Groot Zundert—was not so free from care. Vincent did not get along with people very well. He was a quiet child but a stubborn and willful one. He suffered long, dark moods that suddenly gave way to bright moments of great happiness. But most of the time there was no middle ground—only these two extremes.

Vincent could not help but be deeply resentful that his parents often compared him to a brother who died one year before his own birth. This earlier child—who had also been named Vincent—lived for only six weeks.

Curiously, they had both been born on March 30, but one year apart. However, the "first" Vincent continued to live in his parents' memory. They were certain the dead brother would have been gentle and obedient unlike Vincent. *He* would have been cheerful and even tempered; Vincent was not. *He* would have attended to his studies; Vincent did not.

It is little wonder that Vincent grew increasingly irritable and rebellious as he grew older. When he could not find an outlet for his emotions within his home, he sought for one outside. It was there, in the Brabant moors and woods, roughhousing with the peasant boys, that Vincent found his keenest pleasure. He seemed to understand these coarse boys better than he did his own family. He was as strong and robust as they. Neither the boys nor their parents minded Vincent's roughness.

The members of his own family were not so understanding. Vincent's father was a Protestant pastor. He was a pious, idealistic, but narrow-minded man. On a small salary he struggled to maintain a middle class standard of living. He wanted his three young daughters, who were born after Vincent, to become proper young ladies. He saw Vincent as a misfit whose habits and manners were a bad influence on them.

Theo, Vincent's younger brother, was also a gentle child. Sensitive and slightly built, he had none of Vincent's rough ways or his robust health. Unlike his sisters, he did not withdraw from Vincent. Instead, he admired the strong body of his older brother and began following him about when only a baby. Later they played together, slept in the same bed together, and confided in each other.

12

*"Remember when that great dog leapt at us
as we ran through the heath long ago..."*

*"I am longing for autumn . . . I love so much, so very much, the effect
of the yellow leaves; the green beech trunks stand out so well against them . . ."*

They had many adventures in the countryside that Vincent loved to explore. But while Theo tired easily and had to return home, Vincent seemed to have inexhaustible reserves of strength. Off into the woods he would run to meet the peasant boys.

In time his parents became concerned about Vincent's manners and bad temper. He seemed to prefer the company of peasants to anyone else. Vincent's mother and father felt they must take some action to assure that their eldest son would become a gentleman. Perhaps it would be best, they reasoned, if he were sent to a school where he would be forced to associate with boys of his own class. Finally, the decision was made. When he was eleven, Vincent was sent to the Jean Provily boarding school not far from Zundert.

Vincent adapted himself to the routine of school life as well as he could. But his tendency to solitariness increased. He found refuge in reading and turned to books on philosophy and religion—many of which were too complex for his young age. During these years his ability to express himself with the written word grew.

As Vincent withdrew from the social life of the school, his interest in religion became stronger. His moral views were growing strict and inflexible. He believed that all men should be treated as equals. He was absolutely certain that no man should expect others to do anything for him that he was able to do for himself. And then—as throughout the rest of his life—he fervently believed that the peasant life was the best model to live by.

Physically the boy of sixteen who returned from the Provily school was strong and muscular. He had learned to write well and was familiar with European literature. But he still did not have the manners of a gentleman. He rarely cared about his appearance and did not often comb the reddish hair on his square shaped head. His fair skin was heavily freckled; his intense, light-blue eyes glittered from beneath jutting brows and a high forehead. No, Vincent *still* did not fit into the middle-class family of Pastor Van Gogh.

But the time had come for Vincent to go off on his own. With rare exceptions most children were already working at the age of sixteen. Vincent's parents looked to his rich uncles to help him get a good job. Three of them had been involved in art galleries, and one—Vincent's namesake—was now a wealthy, retired man without any children of his own.

Uncle Cent—as he was affectionately nicknamed—said that he would be glad to help young Vincent on his way in the business world. He arranged for his nephew to be hired as an assistant at Goupil & Co.— a prominent art gallery in The Hague. Goupil & Co. was one of the most successful art galleries in Europe; its main office was in Paris and it maintained branches in several big cities. This seemed like an excellent opportunity for a young man about to make his way in the world. With high hopes Vincent left home in July 1869 for the capital city of the Netherlands.

"*What is drawing? How does one learn it? It is working through an invisible iron wall that seems to stand between what one feels and what one can do.*"

"I feel a power in me
which I must develop, a fire
that I may not quench
but must keep ablaze…"

2. MANY FALSE STARTS

For a boy who had spent all his life in a small country village, the bustling city of The Hague was an exciting place to be. Vincent explored the busy streets, the museums and colorful market places. When he tired of roaming the city, he visited his Aunt Sophy and her two daughters. Since both girls were in love with artists, there was much talk about the world of art.

In the daytime, when he was at his job, the talk of art continued. Here Vincent was surrounded by the kinds of paintings that were popular with the public of this time; there were sunsets, military studies, still lifes, and paintings which told anecdotal stories about daily life.

Vincent worked hard and was well liked by Mr. Tersteeg, the manager. But when he was transferred to the London branch of Goupil & Co., and later to the Paris headquarters, his old problems began to reappear. He did not get along well with either the employees or the customers. At times he became so irritable that he actually argued with the customers about their choices.

As before, Vincent sought refuge in reading. He loved Charles Dickens, George Eliot, and Thomas Carlyle. But his favorite reading was the Bible. For him, the Bible was not only sacred scripture and great literature—it was also *the* indispensable guide for the conduct of daily life. Vincent was firmly convinced that worship in a church was only a very small part of a truly religious life.

When news about Vincent's difficulties reached home, his parents worried about his future. How could he be a success at anything if he could not get along with people? They tried to help him as did Uncle Cent.

But Vincent would not allow himself to be helped. He grew more dissatisfied with each passing week. Eventually he told his employers that he thought it was a sin to make money by selling art. The Goupil & Co.'s patience came to an end. They decided they no longer required the services of Vincent Van Gogh, paid him a month's wages in advance, and asked him to leave.

Vincent took a job teaching French in a boys' boarding school near London. When the headmaster told him the school did not have enough money to pay Vincent his salary, he took a position at a different school. But soon he realized that this too was a mistake. Where could he go now? How could he earn a living? Vincent brooded about his future. His days were given over to reading and walking.

During these walks in London he began to see a side of life he had never known before. The poverty in the East End of London was grim and terrible. Here poor Englishmen, foreigners, sailors, and wanderers lived in one of the world's worst slums. And suddenly it became clear to Vincent that he must devote his life to working with the poor—in the East End of London or wherever he might best serve. This was a

"The most admirable thing I know in the domain of architecture is a rural cottage with a moss-covered thatched roof and a blackened chimney."

wonderful opportunity to do God's work *in the world*. It was a way that he could serve God by serving His children. Vincent determined to become a preacher as soon as possible.

Impatient to begin, Vincent returned to the Netherlands. He began the study of Greek, algebra, and geometry but had great difficulty in mastering these subjects. To Theo he wrote that he was working "as patiently as a dog gnawing a bone." And whenever it became too painful to study, he made little sketches—a habit he had developed long ago. Often these were included in the letters he sent to Theo.

Only two months after he began his studies in Amsterdam, Vincent decided that he would never be able to complete the six-year course. Instead, he was admitted to a small Evangelical school in Brussels. But here, too, he found serious problems awaiting him.

Vincent would not accept criticism from his teachers. He refused to be disciplined and was thought to be sullen and unmanageable. As he sought refuge in art, the sketches which he sent to Theo became more numerous. Looking at art and drawing gave him more pleasure than any other activity. "What beauties art has to offer us!" he wrote. "Provided we remember what we see, we need never be empty, or really lonely, or ever alone."

When Vincent finished his training, he was not an ordained minister but a lay preacher who was allowed to perform religious services without official status in the church. But the Evangelical Council, which seriously doubted his abilities, refused to assign him a ministry. He

22

"*Now I am again in such a period of struggle and discouragement, of patience and impatience, of hope and desolation…*"

*"Only if I study drawing this
seriously and thoroughly, always
trying to portray truly what
I see, shall I arrive…"*

was bitterly disappointed but remained determined. And yet—what was he to do? Where could he best find a way to serve?

Then Vincent remembered reading about life in the Belgian coal mining country. Here, as in the East End of London, human beings lived in terrible poverty and hardship. Vincent asked to be sent as a missionary without pay to the Borinage—the coal mining region of southern Belgium.

Both living and working conditions in the Borinage were worse than he expected. The poor men who worked in these mines were paid too little to feed their families. They worked twelve hours a day in the dark, foul-smelling mines. The villages they lived in were grim and ugly. But perhaps the most terrible thing about life in the Borinage was the fact that four to five thousand children under the age of fourteen were forced to work in the mines.

For two years Vincent attempted to relieve the misery of the miners' lives. He not only preached the gospel but tried to be of practical help. When a fire broke out in the mines, Vincent went among the injured and dying giving comfort and dressing wounds. He gave away his money and clothes. He lived in worse poverty than some of the miners.

But such selflessness is unusual. Soon people began to suspect Vincent's good intentions. He was *too* devoted, *too* intense. The Evangelical Council was not accustomed to seeing their ministers sleeping on the floors of huts or eating crusts of bread—both of which Vincent insisted upon doing. He was warned that he *must* change his ways.

Vincent's ways could not change but his *ideas* about religion were changing. In his letters home he spoke less about his sermons and more about his work with the ill or injured. Gradually his attention was turning to the terrible social and economic injustices he saw around him. When the miners went out on strike after a serious mine explosion, Vincent supported them. He was outraged at the mine owners who refused to give the miners adequate pay or to improve their working conditions.

This defiant act toward authority and land ownership was too much for the Evangelical Council. In July of 1879 they sent notice of his dismissal. Although he was given three months to find another job, he left the Borinage at once.

A time of great suffering now began for Vincent. He wandered barefoot through the grim countryside. He slept in the open and was almost totally dependent on the kindness of strangers. Some, who were moved to pity for the strange wanderer, gave him crusts of bread and soup in exchange for his sketches.

Now he was drawing more and more. He felt a great need to express his feelings about the sadness, and the beauty, of life around him. Drawing the peasants and their somber countryside helped to satisfy this need. Vincent continued to send his drawings to Theo who saw that his brother was growing as an artist. He encouraged him to continue.

Vincent was now twenty-seven. He had tried to be an art dealer, a teacher, and a minister. He had failed at each. But Vincent was well aware of the deep problems which impeded his success. To Theo he

26

*"I am always filled
with remorse, terribly so,
when I think of my work
that is so little in harmony
with what I should
have liked to do."*

"*Believe me, I work, I drudge, I grind all day long, and I do so with pleasure; but I should get very discouraged if I could not go on working as hard or even harder.*"

wrote, "Whatever I do, I do not inspire confidence. How then could I be useful in any way to anyone? . . . I am very easily swayed by passions. I am capable of doing—indeed I am likely to do—things which are more or less mad and which I am usually somewhat sorry for afterwards. Now, bearing this in mind, what am I to do? Ought I to consider myself a dangerous fellow, incapable of doing anything worthwhile? I do not think so. My job is to put my own passions to some good use."

The way was clear now. Vincent was convinced that he must persist in doing that which gave him such great pleasure. He could hardly do otherwise, for his need to express himself was too great. Henceforward, Vincent determined to devote his life to art.

"I am in a rage of work," Vincent wrote soon afterward. His great need to find an expression of his passionate emotions had been restrained for too long. Now they poured out in a torrent of work. He drew the miners at work and at rest. He sketched the miserable huts they lived in. He copied the works of the masters he admired. Foremost among these were Rembrandt and Jean François Millet.

Theo—who was now working as an art dealer in Paris—continued to encourage him. He not only sent him pictures and books but money which he saved from his own small salary. The more he worked, the more Vincent became convinced that he must have formal art training in an art school. But when he arrived in Brussels in the fall of 1880, he found that he was too poor to enroll in the academy.

Instead, he found an artist who taught him some of the basic rules of perspective. He also gave Vincent a book on anatomy. As soon as

Vincent rented a small garret room, he began to teach himself to draw the human figure.

He was too poor to buy much beside bread, chestnuts, fruit, and soup. And he was desperately lonely. He longed for the security and familiarity of his parents' home. When they gave their permission for his return, he packed his things and set out for Etten, the small Dutch village to which his father had been transferred.

Vincent continued with his work. Every morning he left the house with his sketchbook. When he returned in the evenings it was filled with drawings. And, as before, it was not the rich or the elegant who interested him, but the poor and struggling—the peasants of the countryside. Why he chose to paint them was a mystery to his parents. Why paint ugliness, they asked, when there was so much beauty in the world?

Discussions grew into arguments. The arguments became violent and Vincent stormed out of the house. His parents' worries grew worse. What were they to do with this extraordinary son of theirs? Even his ragged, shabby appearance, untidy red beard and hair caused them embarrassment. When Vincent began to argue with his father about religion, the tension grew much worse.

Their arguments came to a climax on Christmas day when Vincent stubbornly refused to go to church. Religion was "horrible," he told his father. He wanted nothing more to do with it. But he knew that his parents could no longer endure these arguments. The day after Christmas Vincent paid a sad good-bye to his mother and father. Once more he set out on his long and lonely path.

*"The great thing
is to gather new
vigor in reality…"*

"So you see that I am in a rage of work, though for the moment it does not produce very brilliant results."

3. THE SEARCH FOR LOVE

Vincent fled to The Hague. He went at once to the house of his cousin and her husband. Anton Mauve was a successful painter. He helped Vincent to find a studio, gave him materials, and encouraged him to work. Vincent accepted Mauve's loan of money but he could not accept the older painter's advice on the study of art. Anton Mauve suggested that Vincent copy plaster casts to improve his knowledge of human anatomy. To Vincent, who had such respect for the living being, the idea seemed outrageous. The two artists argued and before long the brief friendship was over.

Once again Vincent was alone. He continued to work and to study paintings in the great museums of The Hague. He was completely dependent on the money that Theo sent him every month. And, as in the past, there was often not enough money for both food and art materials. He never hesitated to sacrifice food. Frequently Vincent went for days with little or nothing to eat. But he never stopped working.

In the evenings he searched for the friendship and love he so desperately needed. Finally he found a woman who seemed to need him as much as he needed her. Her name was Christine but Vincent called her Sien, meaning *his own*. "She is not young, nor beautiful," Vincent wrote Theo. "She is rather tall and strongly built. Her hands are not the hands of a lady . . . but the hands of one who works hard."

The woman had been a prostitute and now she was pregnant. Her skin was slightly pockmarked and she was far from beautiful. She used obscene language and had an uncontrollable temper. But she needed love and kindness; at this crucial point in her life she needed someone to care for both herself and her child who was about to be born. Vincent was drawn irresistibly by the opportunity to serve humanity in the form of this poor woman.

"Thank God," he wrote Theo, "I have been able thus far to protect her from cold and by sharing my bread with her. . . . I want to marry this woman to whom I am attached and who is attached to me. I want to go through the joys and sorrows of the domestic life in order to paint them from my own experience. . . . One feels best what love is when sitting near a sick bed, sometimes without a cent of money in one's pocket. It is not a gathering of strawberries in the spring."

Throughout her pregnancy Vincent nursed Sien. When the baby was ready to be born, he took her to a maternity hospital in Leyden. The fact that the child was illegitimate meant nothing to Vincent. He saw only two human beings who needed help and love; he was determined to give these as fully as he was capable of giving them. "I intend to marry this woman," he wrote Theo. ". . . Nobody cared for her or wanted her; she was alone and forsaken; and I have taken her up and given her all the love, all the tenderness, all the care that was in me."

34

*"She had had many cares,
one could see that,
and life had been
hard on her..."*

But sensing that Theo would not be pleased by his plans to marry, he first asked his brother's opinion.

Theo immediately sent his disapproval. He wrote that such a marriage would be a terrible blow to Vincent's parents. And he pointed out that it was financially impossible. Vincent could barely live on the small allowance that Theo sent him; how could he possibly support a wife and child as well?

Vincent replied that come what may, he *must* marry Sien. He said that the fact that she had given birth to a child "takes away all the stain from her. I respect a woman who is a mother."

Once again the patient, loving Theo kept silent and sent Vincent a hundred and fifty francs. Vincent accepted the money gratefully but Theo's disapproval remained in his mind; he hesitated about going through with his plans for marriage.

He busied himself with buying furnishings for their small apartment and began to care for his new family which now included a young son. He tended the mother, washed the baby, dressed it, and delighted in playing with it. But within months the relationship between Vincent and Sien began to break apart. No one had ever found Vincent easy to get along with. Sien, too, had a temper that flared up at the slightest provocation. Poverty and hunger created problems and these problems led to serious quarrels. Finally Vincent and Sien decided to go their separate ways.

Although the decision was of Vincent's own making, once he was alone a great wave of depression came over him. He became convinced

"*Is it a sin to love, to need love, not to be able
to live without love? I think a life without love
is a sinful and immoral condition.*"

"You [Theo] are kind to painters and I tell you, the more
I think it over, the more I feel that there is nothing
more truly artistic than to love people."

that he was a burden to his brother and that he caused pain to everyone he met. In the midst of his great unhappiness he wrote to Theo that "Life has the color of dishwater. On such days one would like to have the company of a friend."

When he returned to his room, the extreme loneliness was overpowering. But he did not let it interfere with his work. Nothing must hinder his growth as a painter. Certainly not the lack of money.

Once, when he found himself totally without money to buy paint, he took ordinary kitchen dye colors, mixed them with grindings from a coffee pot, and used these instead of paint. Long ago he had given up caring about his clothes. Of these, he wrote Theo, ". . . I wear what has been given me; I have worn clothes from father and you which sometimes do not fit as they should because of the difference in our sizes."

In the fall of 1883 Vincent decided to leave The Hague. Tiring of city life, he set out for the province of Drenthe where his wish was "to live for a time with a peasant, far away in the country, far away, alone with nature."

After a few days of exploration Vincent set to painting landscapes of the heath that he found "inexpressibly beautiful." His experience with the inhabitants added to his conviction that he had "a certain hardiness in common with the peasants." And yet he felt the same pattern of difficulties and frustrations dogging his steps.

To Theo he wrote, "You remember, perhaps, how it was with me in the Borinage? Well, I am rather afraid it will be the same thing all over again. I did not see any good at the time, nor do I now, of coming to such a point of destitution, of actually having no roof over my head, of having to wander and wander forever like a tramp . . ."

But by late autumn the need to leave Drenthe and wander again overwhelmed Vincent. He set out on a six-hour walk to Nuenen where his father had been transferred.

Vincent was given the laundry room, which was separate from the house, as his studio. Once again he worked in the fields and in the homes of the peasants. Through the long cold winter he made many sketches of weavers at their looms. Later the sketches were used as starting points for paintings.

When spring came, Vincent drew the peasants plowing the potato fields. The natural beauty of the peasants' way of life fascinated him. To observe was not enough; he wanted to know their lives as intimately as they themselves did. To Theo he wrote, "One must paint the peasants as being one of them, as feeling, thinking as they do."

During this period Vincent completed one of his first major paintings. The picture, "The Potato Eaters," was first sketched by Vincent as he sat in the corner of a room and watched a family of peasants eat their supper. "The Potato Eaters" was finished in the spring of 1885. In a mood of exultation Vincent wrote Theo, "It will perhaps disappoint you . . . but . . . it comes from the heart of the peasant's life. . . . I have loved to make it and I have often worked at it with a certain animation."

Although pleased with progress in his work, Vincent was not happy with his home life. Difficulties with his parents were growing worse. This shabby man with an explosive temper did not fit into their clean,

*"I have to observe
and draw everything
that belongs to
country life…
I no longer stand
helpless before nature,
as I used to…"*

well-run home. They had tolerated his emotional outbursts for a long time but they could no longer deal with him. For the first time Vincent sensed that he was no longer welcome in his parents' home. Although not a word was said, he knew his parents wanted him to leave. Vincent wrote Theo that their parents "felt the same dread taking me in as they would a big rough dog."

The time had come to move on. And Vincent welcomed the idea of living in a city again. He needed the stimulation of going to museums and seeing other artists at work. He also needed models, which were no longer available to him at Nuenen. Most artists were under suspicion during these years simply because their lives did not conform to the accepted ways. This, coupled with Vincent's odd behavior and uncontrollable temper, led the villagers to malicious gossip about the artist and his models. When it reached the ears of the Roman Catholic priest, he forbade the villagers to pose for Vincent. The artist found this absolutely intolerable.

In November of 1885 Vincent crossed the border into Belgium. Antwerp, where he settled, was a busy port city; searching through the harbor cafés and dance halls, he was delighted by the many colorful types of human beings he found there. He also joined the Académie des Beaux Arts and was told once again that he should spend at least a year drawing from plaster casts.

He was often close to starvation. During his first six weeks in Antwerp he lived almost entirely on bread; throughout this period he had only six hot meals. When Theo sent some extra money, Vincent bought a proper meal and then found he could not digest it. His teeth became broken and decayed. Reluctantly he went to a doctor who told him that he was having an "absolute breakdown."

Vincent had always been strong physically and he was frightened by this illness; and suddenly he was tired of Antwerp, tired of always being alone. A great desire to see Theo came over him. Theo begged him to wait for a while; he said he was not ready for him yet. But Vincent needed desperately to move on. And the desire to be with his brother was overpowering. He took the train for Paris—never to return north again.

"*I draw, not to annoy people, but to amuse them, or to make them see things that are worth observing and which not everybody knows.*"

4. A NEW BEGINNING

After recovering from the first shock of seeing his gaunt, weakened brother, Theo took firm measures to return him to health as soon as possible. Vincent's decayed teeth were pulled out and replaced by a set of false ones. Theo bought him some new clothes and watched with pleasure as Vincent's strength gradually returned.

The apartment Theo was living in did not have room for a studio so he moved to another, larger apartment in Montmartre. It had beautiful views of Paris and was cleaned daily by a maid. Vincent was pleased with his new living arrangements and it seemed that he would adjust well to life in Paris.

In a mood of optimism Theo wrote his parents, "You would not recognize Vincent, he makes great progress in his work, he is in better spirits and many people like him. . . . If we can go on living together like this, I think the most difficult time is over and he will make his own way."

Theo seemed justified in having such high hopes. Vincent was busy meeting the artists of Paris and learning more about that new school of painting that was receiving so much attention—Impressionism. Vincent had known about Impressionism for several years but he considered it a temporary fashion. Now, he was delighted by these bright, light-filled canvases that were the talk of Paris.

The Impressionists believed that painters had never before captured the great brilliance of sunlight on nature. To achieve this end they used many strokes of pure bright color next to each other. The forms of an object were lightly and rapidly sketched and emphasis was placed on painting out of doors. Theo, too, had great respect for the Impressionist painters. On the second floor of the gallery where he worked he regularly displayed the works of Monet, Renoir, and other prominent Impressionists.

For a time Theo and Vincent got along very well indeed. Vincent was busy with his work during the day and in the evening he discussed art with the painters who had become his friends. He always carried pieces of colored chalk to illustrate his theories. Whatever flat surface was available—a tablecloth or a white wall—would become his drawing surface. But Vincent came home late at night so over-stimulated that he kept Theo up talking excitedly about his views.

Friends began to see that Theo was paying a heavy price for Vincent's happiness. When the weather was cold and Vincent was forced to remain inside, their arguments grew worse. Vincent was still a very difficult person to live with and Theo had to swallow many of the strong words that came to his lips. Now his health was beginning to suffer because of it. Theo was torn between wanting his brother to stay and asking him to leave.

"The grapes are magnificent this year because of the fine autumn weather..."

Meanwhile, Vincent was working at a brisk pace. His canvases were changing greatly. Gone were the somber, dark colors of the north. Instead, a fresh, bright sunlight illuminated them. The scenes of Montmartre all showed the Impressionist influence. The portraits, too, were radically different. During this time Vincent completed twenty self-portraits.

On fine days he set out with a big canvas on his back, his arms loaded with paints and collapsible easel. He explored the quiet parks, the banks of the Seine, and the colorful restaurants. The furious manner with which he attacked his canvas amazed people who paused to watch.

During this time Père Tanguy sat for his portrait as he had also sat for other great painters of his time. This old man, who kept an art supplies shop, was a revolutionary both in art and politics. He not only showed the Impressionist painters but provided a meeting place where they could gather for discussions. He was a generous person who allowed the artists to buy canvas, paint, and brushes on credit. Père Tanguy saw at once that Vincent was a great artist and encouraged him to come to the shop whenever he liked. He hung Vincent's paintings on the walls.

Vincent's portrait of Père Tanguy subtly conveys the old man's kindliness and simplicity. The background consists of Japanese prints which were popular then in Paris and greatly admired by Vincent.

Theo watched with pleasure as Vincent's canvases grew in power and originality. But he could not endure the constant squabbling with

"In spite of everything I shall rise again; I will take
up my pencil, which I have forsaken in my great discouragement
and I will go on with my drawing."

*"It is splendid to look at something and admire it,
to think about it and keep hold of it, and then to say
I am going to draw and work at it until
I have it fixed on paper."*

his brother. He went to the Netherlands for a visit, to find some relief. When he returned, he found that Vincent had turned the apartment into a shambles. Paintings were everywhere; the disorder was complete. Within a few days Theo was writing, "My home life is almost unbearable. I wish he would go and live by himself. He talks of it sometimes, but if I were to suggest it, he would at once give up the idea. All I ask is that he leave me alone, but that's the very thing he never does. I can hardly stand it."

But Vincent, too, had considered the possibility of leaving Paris. He began to talk of founding a school of Impressionists—"a community of painters" in the south of France. By their combined efforts they would carry painting into new experimental ground. Vincent proposed this idea to several artists but it was Gauguin, above all, whom he hoped would join him in this new venture.

Vincent was not the only one to be drawn to the extraordinary and magnetic figure of Gauguin. Although his work had not yet found a market, he had a circle of admirers and followers. Paul Gauguin had been a prosperous stockbroker and a respected member of the community; he was a married man with a family to support. Yet he gave up his business and left his wife and children so that he might devote the rest of his life to art.

Gauguin refused Vincent's offer but Vincent had no intention of giving up his plan. There were other reasons why he wanted to leave Paris. He was longing for the warmth and brilliant light of the south. Toulouse-Lautrec had told him of a charming town in Provence where

51

"As long as autumn lasts I shall not have hands, canvas, and colors enough to paint the beautiful things I see."

one could live cheaply. And the old desire for the countryside and for peasant life were welling up again.

He was weary of Paris and the friends he had made there. "As men," he told Theo, "they disgust me." Theo was busy with his personal life; he was contemplating marriage and soon might have new responsibilities. Père Tanguy's wife began scolding him for being too generous toward Vincent. The result was that Vincent felt himself drifting toward depression again. ". . . And at times I already feel old and broken. . . . To succeed one needs ambition, and ambition seems to me absurd."

Yes, Vincent definitely needed a change of scene to refuel his creative fires. And where could he find new horizons of brilliant sunlight and fascinating new types to paint? In the South of France of course. South, *south*—the idea of moving southward became an obsession.

In February 1888, Vincent set out for Provence.

"The great thing is to give the sun and the blue sky their
full force and brilliance, and the scorched—and often melancholy—
fields the delicate aroma of thyme..."

5. THE SOUTH OF FRANCE

When Vincent stepped off the train in Arles, he was surprised to find snow glittering in the bright sunlight. But here, unlike Paris, the skies were a deep, radiant blue. In a few days the snow melted and fresh, green buds appeared on the trees. Soon the air grew warm and smelled of sweet blossoms.

Vincent had never seen such wonderful flowering fruit trees and bright, unfamiliar flowers. In a mood of delight he wrote Theo that the sight of the blossoming almond trees was "an intoxicating vision."

During the first weeks in Arles Vincent was much happier than he had been in Paris. "What an opportunity," he wrote, ". . . nature here is so extraordinarily beautiful. It's the chance of a lifetime! I feel a different man from the one who came here. I let myself go, paint what I see and just how I feel—and hang the rules."

Vincent loved the ancient town of Arles and the appearance of the townspeople. He wanted to paint everything—the charming streets, the buildings, and the men and women. But, as before, the overpowering beauty of the countryside drew him into the fields.

He set up his easel in the midst of the blossoming fruit orchards and painted a series of canvases that expressed his joy in the coming of spring. He worked quickly and produced a large amount of work—perhaps *too* much, he sometimes feared. "I am using a tremendous lot of colors and canvases," he wrote Theo, "but I hope it isn't a waste of money. I want to paint . . . an orchard of astounding gaiety."

When the *mistral*—a cold, strong, northeast wind—began to blow in the early spring, Vincent did not let it stop his work outdoors. Although the wind coated his canvases with dust and sometimes with small pebbles, he persisted in working in the open. Often the *mistral* blew with such great force that he had to work with one hand while holding down the canvas with the other.

But it was the vibrant brilliance of the sun which, more than anything else, excited Vincent. "I work even during the hour of noon," he wrote, ". . . in the glaring sun, without a scrap of shade in the cornfields, and believe me I am happy as a cricket. Heavens, why did I not get to know this country when I was twenty-five years of age instead of arriving here at thirty-five!"

With his easel strapped to his back, he trudged to the fields each morning. He usually spent the entire day working out of doors. If the wind blew dust over his work, if insects swarmed around his face, if he didn't take time to eat—it didn't matter. All that mattered was bringing home a good painting in the evening.

But evening is the time, after a day of solitary work, that an artist needs friends and companionship. Vincent made very few friends in Arles. The best, by far, was the kindly postman, Roulin.

Roulin sat for a portrait that became one of Vincent's finest paintings. In it he captured the slightly tense quality which many people

56

*"You see, when one
is getting old,
one must really
rule out illusions…"*

express when they sit for a portrait. Roulin's face, with its enormous square beard and open expression, verifies Vincent's description of him as "A good sort . . . so wise and so full of feeling and so trustful."

Roulin would not accept money for his modeling but he did allow Vincent to pay for his dinner one night at the café. Of him Vincent wrote to Theo, "although [he] is not quite old enough to be like a father to me, he has the same gentleness and tenderness for me that an old soldier might have for a young one."

But Roulin, good friend that he was, could not offer Vincent stimulating conversation about art. Vincent's thoughts turned often to his old dream of forming a colony of forward-thinking artists. Another check from Theo brought this dream closer to fulfillment. Vincent rented a house that was "painted yellow outside, whitewashed inside and full of sunshine." His studio on the ground floor had a red-tiled floor and freshly painted white walls. There were two bedrooms on the second floor. The yellow house, on the Place Lamartine, appears in several of Vincent's pictures.

Vincent did not have enough money to buy furniture for the new house. He worked there in the daytime but continued to sleep in his room over the café. One of his first models in the new house was a dark-skinned soldier who wore the colorful uniform of the French North African troops called Zouaves. Vincent placed the dark-skinned soldier on a stool in a corner of his studio. The youthful masculinity of the soldier easily overcame the fanciness of his uniform. Vincent wrote, "It's a savage combination of tones . . . not easy to manage . . .

"There will be my bedroom which I want extremely simple but with large, solid furniture..."

*"It is fun to work in rather wild places, where one
has to dig one's easel in between the stones lest
the wind should blow the whole caboodle over."*

but all the same I should like always to be working on common, even loud portraits like this." The young soldier, he added, "had the neck of a bull and the eye of a tiger."

Vincent tried to lure Gauguin from Brittany, where he was now living, with wonderful descriptions of Arles and its people. But Gauguin hesitated. He had very little money and considerable doubts about living with this unpredictable, excitable Dutchman. While Gauguin slowly made up his mind, Vincent continued to produce paintings at a furious pace.

Throughout the spring he painted bareheaded in the outdoors. As summer approached, the burning intensity of the sun forced him to buy a large straw hat. He used it constantly and it appears in some of his most magnificent self-portraits. The heat grew oppressive but Vincent never complained. Now his praise of the brilliant summer sun reached its peak.

He said that the intense light of the south brought him "a terrible lucidity at moments, these days when nature is so beautiful, I am not conscious of myself any more and the picture comes to me as in a dream." In a moment of "extraordinary exultation" he cried, "Life is after all enchanted."

But such delight was always a forerunner of Vincent's depressive states. With the coming of autumn his spirits began to sink again. "I have had a very thin time of it these days," he wrote in September 1888. "I have done absolutely nothing but paint and sleep." For four days he did not have money enough for food so he lived on bread and coffee. When he could not pay the rent, he asked the owner to accept paintings of the hotel in exchange for the room rent.

The owner agreed so Vincent painted a picture of the café which occupied the ground floor of the hotel. It remained open throughout the night and was a place of refuge for people who had nowhere else to sleep.

Vincent entitled this painting "The Night Cafe." He wrote Theo that it was "one of the ugliest pictures I have ever done. . . . I have tried to express, as it were, the powers of darkness in a low wine shop, and all this in an atmosphere like a devil's furnace of pale sulphur."

A sour, lemon-yellow light shines from four hanging lamps above the green-topped billiard table. The clock above the door reads fifteen minutes past midnight. The men who are sleeping at the tables by the wall bury their heads in their arms. And the white-coated owner has green hair—a detail which appears to emphasize the fatigue and desolation of the early morning hours.

Fatigue, lack of food, and the late summer heat began to press in on Vincent. In his letters to Theo he began to speak more openly of the possibility of his madness. And the loneliness, the unbearable loneliness, was almost more than he could endure. He was not only an outcast in Arles but a figure of such curiosity that some of the young people pointed at him as they gossiped about his oddities. Would Gauguin *never* come to join him? Vincent longed for his companionship. Despair was overtaking him when a letter arrived from Theo with the long-awaited news.

"Ideas for my work are coming to me in swarms, so that though I'm alone, I have no time to think or feel, I go on painting like a steam engine…"

"And what am I?
Only a man who has
difficult, trying work
to do, for which
he needs quiet and
peace and sympathy."

6. LIFE WITH GAUGUIN

The news was indeed wonderful! On October 23 Theo had sold one of Gauguin's paintings. With the money Gauguin would be able to buy a ticket to Arles and spend several months with Vincent. He had decided definitely to come and would soon be on his way.

Vincent's spirits soared as he awaited the friend he so greatly admired. He proudly showed Gauguin's photograph to Roulin and some other friends. With great impatience he spoke of his friend's imminent arrival and then rushed back to the yellow house to prepare it for him.

Gauguin arrived during the night, spent the last few hours of darkness at the café, and knocked on Vincent's door at sunrise. After a warm embrace Vincent showed him around his beloved yellow house. Gauguin found the second floor was tolerable but was shocked at the disorder of the studio and the kitchen.

He took off his jacket, got to work, and within a few hours had the rooms clean and shining. He decided that Vincent could not handle money with care, so he suggested a plan to deal with the problem. The painters would get three different boxes. One would contain the money for their food, the other money for rent; the last box would hold money for entertainment. Gauguin explained that whenever money was taken from a box, a note giving the reason should be left inside.

Vincent was delighted by such a sensible idea. Almost everything that Gauguin did seemed to please Vincent during the first weeks of their life together. Gauguin knew how to cook and prepared delicious meals. Vincent ate them with a double pleasure as he realized how much money could be saved by dining at home.

Within days Vincent was writing Theo that Gauguin ". . . is an astonishing man." He said that he was ". . . thankful not to be alone. . . . It does me an enormous amount of good to have a companion as intelligent as Gauguin and to watch him at work."

Gauguin accepted Vincent's admiration as something he fully deserved. He was used to praise from his admirers and disciples. Gauguin was far more worldly than Vincent had ever been. He was self-confident and used to getting his own way. When he wanted models, he went out in the streets of Arles and found them—unlike Vincent who had such difficulty in getting people to sit for him. And Gauguin, too, was pleased with his new companion. He had thought of Vincent as a difficult, eccentric person. Instead, he found an idealistic man who tried to live by his ethical and moral beliefs.

During the first weeks of their life together Vincent's delight knew no bounds. Optimistically he wrote to Theo, "I dare to predict that in six months Gauguin and you and I will see that a studio has been founded that will endure—a useful maybe even essential outpost for all who want to paint in the south."

But this happiness was not to last for long. Six weeks after Gauguin's

*"I purposely bought
a mirror good enough
to enable me to work
from my own image in
default of a model…"*

arrival the first problems in their relationship began to appear. During wet or windy days when the artists could not work out of doors, they painted in the yellow house. There was also much time for long talks about art and artists. But what began as a friendly discussion often turned into a heated and bitter argument.

Gauguin had no regard for many of the painters whom Vincent admired. But Vincent could not bear to hear Gauguin speak against them. As he defended his favorites, he lost control of himself and raged against his friend. Gauguin found these outbursts irritating and time-consuming. And he was becoming a little bored with Arles.

When he spoke about leaving Provence, Vincent became alarmed. Their constant arguments were painful but not nearly as painful as the loneliness that would return if Gauguin left. And yet, Vincent could do nothing to stop their quarrels which were becoming more intense and more exhausting.

When Gauguin completed his portrait of Vincent, events took a turn for the worse. Vincent looked at the painting for a long time before speaking. He saw that Gauguin had skillfully caught his likeness and his fiery emotional nature. But the painting was disturbing to him. ". . . it's me all right," Vincent reluctantly agreed, ". . . but me mad."

Soon Gauguin was writing to Theo that he respected Vincent's intelligence but that he and Vincent were too unlike in temperament to live together harmoniously. He was convinced that they would never be able to get along; Gauguin asked Theo to send him enough money so that he might return to Paris.

68

*"I am very glad that
my drawing is improving,
it gives me courage.
Drawing is the principle thing,
whatever they may say,
and it is the most
difficult, too."*

"There is a sun, a light, that for want of a better word I can only call yellow, pale sulphur yellow, pale golden citron. How lovely yellow is!"

Vincent pleaded with Gauguin to remain. He promised that he would try to control his emotions. But within a day or two the artists were involved in another raging argument. Vincent said, "Our discussions become *excessively electric.*"

Later that evening Vincent and Gauguin went to the café. As soon as the wine was served, Vincent picked up his glass and threw it at Gauguin's face. Fortunately it missed him.

But Vincent's violent and erratic act also alarmed him. Gauguin was now convinced that something was seriously wrong with Vincent. Taking him firmly by the arm he led him out of the café and took him home. Gauguin put him to bed where he fell into a deep sleep immediately.

The next morning Vincent said that he did not know what he was doing when he threw the glass. He apologized to Gauguin and begged him to stay with him. Gauguin remained firm. He said that it was impossible for him to stay in the little yellow house with Vincent. It would be far more sensible, he explained calmly, if he left before more serious trouble developed between them.

Vincent's heart sank. Gauguin was leaving him! He brooded darkly all though the day. That evening, as Gauguin crossed the Place Lamartine, he heard quick, short footsteps following rapidly. He turned around and saw Vincent coming at him with an open razor gleaming in his hand.

Gauguin spoke sharply and Vincent immediately turned away. He went back to the house and stood before the mirror that he used so often for self-portraits. Then he cut off the lobe of his left ear, and put it into an envelope. As soon as he could stop the flow of blood, he wrapped a scarf around his head and left the house.

Vincent walked to the brothel and handed the envelope to one of the prostitutes. When she opened it up and saw what was inside she fainted. The brothel was in an uproar.

At that point the faithful Roulin appeared. He had been worried about Vincent for weeks. He gently led Vincent back to his house, put him to bed, and tended the wound.

The next morning Gauguin arrived at the house to collect his things before leaving for Paris. He had spent the night in a hotel on the far side of town as a precaution. As soon as he discovered what Vincent had done to himself, he wired Theo to come as soon as possible.

Theo rushed to take the first train to Provence and found his brother in a deep depression. He immediately arranged for Vincent's admittance to a hospital, where a time of great agony began. During the day, when the painter was awake, he was horrified by the wild thoughts that raced through his mind. But sleep was worse. He was the victim of nightmares and would wake up screaming with fear.

He asked to see Gauguin but Gauguin would not visit him. He believed that his presence would excite Vincent too much; although Vincent begged him to come, Gauguin never saw him again. Theo remained with his brother as long as possible. When he left, Gauguin joined him on the return journey to Paris.

Theo hated to leave his brother. Vincent had lost a great deal of blood and was still in danger. And who would look after him? "He has suffered and struggled more than most," Theo wrote. "If he dies my heart will break."

72

"Either shut me up in a madhouse right away— and I shan't oppose it, for I may be deceiving myself—or let me work with all my strength."

"It is a painter's duty to be entirely absorbed by nature..."

7. LAST YEARS

While Vincent remained in the hospital, Roulin came to see him and comfort him as much as possible. Gradually Vincent grew stronger. He was impatient to leave the hospital and begin work again. Vincent wanted to believe that his self-mutilation was a temporary weakness that would not return. To Theo he wrote, "I hope I have been the victim of nothing worse than an artist's prank."

On January 7, 1889, Vincent was given permission to leave the hospital. He rejoiced at the thought of returning to the yellow house that he loved so much. As a celebration Vincent and Roulin had dinner together in a restaurant. Only one piece of bad news marred the happy event; Roulin was to be transferred to Marseilles. Roulin —Vincent's only friend, his supporter, defender, the only person in Arles who understood him—would be leaving him. And this at one of the most critical periods in Vincent's life.

At first Vincent began to paint with uncertainty. But when he returned to an unfinished portrait of Madame Roulin, his confidence and enthusiasm grew stronger. He became fascinated with this portrait, which he called "La Berceuse," and painted it five times. He also did two self-portraits; one of them he entitled "Portrait of the Artist with a Mutilated Ear."

Vincent wanted to use other models but now, even more than before, the people of Arles shrank from him. They all knew of his self-mutilation and thought of him as a strange and perhaps dangerous eccentric. They were no longer content to point their fingers at him but openly called him names and jeered at him.

Boys climbed up to watch through the windows as he painted his own portrait. To them it seemed like a very weird thing to do; as they watched they made faces, mocked Vincent, and accused him of being a madman.

He endured their taunting as long as he could. But the time came when he could stand it no longer. One day he rushed to the window, threw it open and screamed out wildly across the Place Lamartine—a horrible scream of fear and alarm and agony.

As quickly as possible Vincent was rushed to the hospital. This time he was put into a separate room and the door was securely locked. For weeks he lay almost motionless and said nothing.

Dr. Salles, a kindly Protestant pastor who came to visit Vincent, finally encouraged him to speak. Vincent told him, "If the police had prevented the children and grown-ups from crowding around my house and climbing the windows as if I were a curious animal, I should have controlled myself and done no harm to anyone." But already, his will to live was slipping away. An ominous note of resignation sounded as he wrote that he must "endure without complaints, that's the lesson I have to learn."

76

*"Of course, when working
one always feels, and
should feel, a kind
of dissatisfaction
with oneself."*

Life had turned into a nightmare for Vincent. Sooner or later, in the past, the nightmare had faded; life became endurable again. Now the nightmare remained with unbearable intensity. Vincent was not allowed to smoke, to drink, or to paint. He was not permitted to go to the yellow house.

Finally these restrictions were relaxed. Vincent's bedroom door was unlocked. He was also given paints and allowed to work in the hospital garden. As he grew stronger and more confident, Vincent asked to return to the yellow house but his doctor advised against it. He explained that the neighbors were alarmed by his behavior; they were fearful of him and would not welcome his return.

Theo suggested that Vincent return to Paris and live with him. But Vincent doubted if he could face the stimulation of Paris at this critical time in his life. "One day, perhaps," he wrote Theo, "but I couldn't stand a big city at present." He still wanted desperately to return to the yellow house but that was impossible.

Even Vincent had begun to doubt his ability to live alone in the future. "I can't face isolation anymore," he wrote, ". . . my head is not steady enough to work at a stretch by myself as I did before. And I dare not risk making any more public scenes, I'm not fit to govern myself and my affairs."

After several consultations, Vincent, his doctors, and Theo decided he should go to the asylum at St. Rémy not far from Arles. But as he watched his things begin taken from the beloved yellow house, his heart sank. An enormous despair overcame him. He wrote to Theo,

*"Under the blue sky the
orange, yellow, red splashes
of the flowers take on
an amazing brilliance..."*

"I cannot stop drawing because I really have a draftsman's fist ... have I ever doubted or hesitated or wavered since the day I began to draw?"

"I thought of how you had given me all these things with such brotherly love, and how you had kept me all these years, and then for me to have to tell you this wretched ending to it all—oh, I can't tell you what I felt!"

Theo answered with great tenderness, "Our fraternity, our love for each other is worth more than all the money I shall ever possess."

At St. Rémy, Vincent was given the privilege of having two rooms to himself. But he was constantly reminded that this was an insane asylum by the heavy bars on the windows. Although the walls were thick, Vincent could hear the mutterings, shriekings, and screaming of the other inmates very well.

At first he was not permitted to paint outside the hospital grounds. After a period of careful observation, the doctor permitted Vincent to go out in the care of a hospital attendant.

Vincent began to paint the gardens and buildings of St. Rémy. Occasionally the inmates would come up to watch what he was doing and then move on. He wrote Theo that they "leave me in peace and are more discreet and polite than, for instance, the good folk of Arles."

Gradually Vincent began to work farther away from the hospital. He painted in the fields as before. Once again the brilliance of the powerful Mediterranean sun began to fascinate him. Its intensity beat down hotly on his head as he worked in the noonday heat. Toward late summer the richness of the season began to overwhelm him. Everywhere he looked he saw the abundance of the southern fields— the ripe, sweet grapes, the brilliantly colorful vegetables and fruits. And still the hot sun beat down mercilessly.

Vincent was working outdoors when a strong wind began to sweep across the fields. Vincent's easel was thrown down, his canvas was blown into the dust. As he dashed after it, the wind blew fiercely around his head. It seemed that the world itself would blow away in the wild, raging force of the wind. Suddenly Vincent lost control and screamed madly into the gale. He screamed until the great wave of emotion passed, then collapsed near his easel. He was carried back to the hospital by an attendant who had gone to look for him.

After recovering from this attack, he sank into a very severe depression. He feared that he would not ever be cured. As he slipped further and further away from life, he wrote with a heartbreaking sense of loss, "If one could resign oneself to suffering and death, surrender one's will and love of self! But I love to paint, to meet people, and to see nature."

And now what remained for him? Only the likelihood of being locked up in an insane asylum. Vincent's thoughts often turned to death. From his barred windows he saw the reapers cutting down the summer corn. This ancient symbol of death fascinated him. He turned again to paintings of the reaper which he had begun and put aside. "In this reaper fighting like mad under the blazing sun to finish his job I see the image of death," he wrote to Theo. A long, lonely winter passed during which Vincent's letters became increasingly somber.

Alarmed by Vincent's decline, Theo begged him to return to Paris. At last a painting had been sold for approximately eighty dollars. But

"[Dr. Gachet] certainly
seems to me as ill
and distraught as you
or me..."

*"If you are
a painter they think
you are either a fool
or a rich man…"*

Vincent did not rejoice. He agreed to come to Paris for a brief visit with Theo, his wife, and the small child who had recently been born. Afterward he planned to go to the village of Auvers, near Paris, where he would be under the care of Dr. Gachet.

Vincent found Auvers very beautiful. He loved its thatched-roof houses and set to work at once. A period of great productivity began; in the two months that Vincent remained in Auvers he completed seventy paintings and thirty-two drawings. Dr. Gachet did not ask Vincent to stay with him but he was hospitable and the two men saw each other frequently. Vincent painted the doctor's portrait and wrote Theo that he saw in the old man's face the "heartbroken expression of our time."

Although Vincent continued to work, he could not prevent himself from falling into despair. "My steps are wavering," he wrote to Theo, "[but] I set to work again, the brush almost slipping from my fingers." Working in the fields he painted canvases which were ominously dark and brooding. He said that when he painted the "vast fields of wheat under troubled skies . . . I did not need to go out of my way to express sadness and extreme loneliness."

But now this extreme had reached unbearable limits. Vincent seriously doubted his ability to withstand another attack of violent emotion. He could not endure the thought that he would always be a burden to Theo. Even painting no longer meant as much to him.

On Sunday, July 27, 1890, Vincent went out to the fields with his easel and paints. He also carried a pistol. On his way back to the village

*"Love is something
so positive, so strong, so
real that it is impossible
for one who loves to take
back that feeling as
it is to take his
own life…"*

he entered a farmyard and shot himself. The bullet had been aimed at the heart but was deflected by the fifth rib.

Theo rushed to Auvers as soon as he received the news. Vincent was conscious when he arrived. Both Theo and Dr. Gachet believed that Vincent's strong constitution would help him to survive. But on Tuesday morning Vincent's condition worsened. He said, in Dutch, "I wish I could go home now," and then he died.

Dr. Gachet planted sunflowers around Vincent's simple grave in the village cemetery. The headstone gives only Vincent's name and the dates of his birth and death. Theo wrote to one of his sisters, "He had no desire to live and he was content, because he had fought unflinchingly for his conviction, which he had tested with the best and noblest who had gone before him. . . . One must acknowledge that he was a great artist; to be a great man often goes hand in hand. Time will bring the honor due him, and many will grieve to think he died so young. . . ."

Theo's own grief was more than his frail health could endure. Within six months he, too, was dead. Many years afterward his widow had his remains transferred to France where now, in the small, silent cemetery of Auvers, the two brothers lie together.

CHRONOLOGY

1852 *March 30:* Vincent Willem I born.

1853 *March 30:* Vincent Willem II, the painter, born.

1864 *October 1:* Vincent goes to Jan Provily's boarding school at Zevenbergen.

1869 *July 30:* Vincent gets a job at Goupil's Galleries in The Hague.

1873 *June 13:* Vincent is sent to work at the London branch of Goupil & Co.

1874 *October:* Vincent is transferred to the Paris branch of Goupil & Co.

1876 *March:* Vincent is dismissed from Goupil & Co.

1876 *April 17:* Vincent takes a job as assistant teacher in a boys' school at Ramsgate near London.

1877 *May 9:* Vincent prepares for entrance examinations to the faculty of theology at the University of Amsterdam.

1878 *December 26:* Vincent leaves for the Borinage, the coal mining district of Belgium.

1880 *August:* Vincent begins to devote all his time to art.

1881 *December 31:* Vincent moves to The Hague.

1883 *December:* Vincent goes to Nuenen where he remains for two years drawing peasant life.

1885 *November:* Vincent lives briefly in Antwerp, Belgium.

1886 *March:* Vincent goes to Paris where he lives with Theo.

1888 *February 20:* Vincent leaves Paris for Arles in Provence.

1888 *September 20:* Gauguin arrives in Arles to live with Vincent.

1888 *December 24:* Vincent cuts off the lobe of his left ear and is hospitalized.

1889 *About May 8:* Of his own free will, Vincent goes to the asylum at St. Rémy de Provence.

1890 *Spring:* At an exhibition in Brussels, a painting of Vincent's is sold for 400 francs—the only one sold during his lifetime.
May 23: Vincent goes to live at Auvers-sur-Oise not far from Paris where he is under the care of Dr. Gachet.
July 27: Vincent shoots himself in the chest.
July 29: Vincent dies at dawn.

FOR FURTHER READING

ANDRIESSE, EMMY. *The World of Van Gogh*. New York: Holbein Publishing Company, 1953.

AUDEN, W. H. *Van Gogh: A Self Portrait. Letters Revealing His Life As a Painter*. Greenwich, Connecticut: New York Graphic Society, 1961.

GRAETZ, H. R. *The Symbolic Language of Vincent Van Gogh*. New York: McGraw-Hill, 1963

HAMMACHER, A. M. *Van Gogh*. London: Paul Hamlyn, 1967.

HULSKER, JAN. *Van Gogh's Diary: The Artist's Life in His Own Words & Art*. New York: William Morrow, 1971.

SHAPIRO, MEYER, ed. *Vincent Van Gogh*. New York: Harry N. Abrams, 1970.

TRALBERT, MARC EDO. *Vincent Van Gogh*. New York: The Viking Press, 1969.

WALLACE, ROBERT. *World of Van Gogh*. New York: Time-Life Books, 1969.

PICTURE CREDITS

INDEX